Resurrection
True or False?

Resurrection
True or False?

BY SPIROS ZODHIATES

AMG PUBLISHERS
CHATTANOOGA, TN 37422

Third printing 1984

In Canada:
Purpose Products
81 Temperence
Aurora, Ont. L46 2R1

Cover Design: Howard Weinstein
Illustrations: Florence Anderson
Copyright 1977 by Spiros Zodhiates
Printed in the United States of America

Dedicated to
Otto and Florence Anderson
in appreciation of their faithful
service with me at
AMG INTERNATIONAL

PREFACE

Resurrection—is it a pious hope, or must we conclude that death ends all? Conjecture will not suffice in such a matter. You owe it to yourself to find out. If you've never really thought about it, why not do so now? This book will help you discover whether anyone in the past ever rose from the dead. If so, it should give you pause, and prevent you from dismissing such a possibility before you've carefully examined it. Historical facts override philosophical speculations based on presuppositions.

Once convinced that resurrection is a fact, you owe it to yourself to find out what's going to happen to you when it does occur. What you will be after the resurrection depends on what you are before you die. It's the part of wisdom to start preparing for that momentous change now. The revelations of the One who rose from the dead will help you adequately to prepare for that day. Can you believe what Christ said in John 5:28, 29: "Marvel not at this: for the hour is coming, in the which all that are in the graves shall hear his voice, and shall come forth; they that have done evil, unto the resurrection of damnation"? What does it all mean? Find out by carefully reading the pages that follow.

—Spiros Zodhiates

CONTENTS

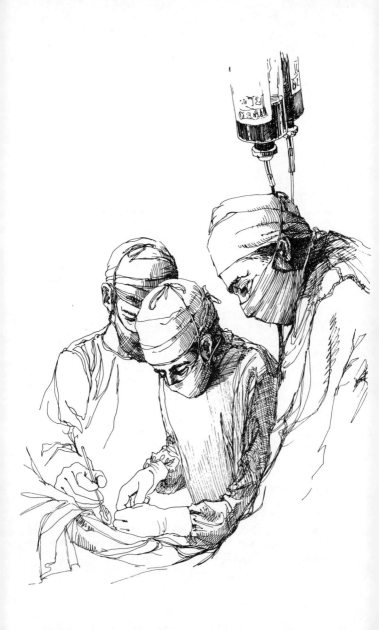

The Man Who Wouldn't Be King

Medical science has made almost unbelievable advances against the ills that beset the human race. Kidney transplants, heart transplants, corneal transplants, pace-makers, and a host of other procedures that would have been considered miracles a short time ago are now becoming almost commonplace.

Yet one thing is still beyond scientific skill, and that is imparting life and consciousness to inert matter—creating life or raising the dead. Only God could do that. Creative intelligence had to be behind the universe and all that you see. No one has yet been able to dispute the fact that out of nothing, nothing can come.

Imagine, then, the excitement if someone came

to your town who could raise the dead. Radio, TV, and all other communications media would flash the news around the world. People would flock to see him from every corner of the globe. We'd all like to meet such a miracle worker.

Yet this actually has happened. The town was Bethany. And the miracle worker was Jesus Christ. Can you imagine what happened when He raised a man named Lazarus who had been dead for three days? The news spread throughout the whole region: "Lazarus, the friend of Jesus, died and was buried, but Jesus brought him back to life!" You can also picture the joy in that home on the following Saturday night, when Christ ate supper with the risen Lazarus and his sisters. How they must have thanked Him over and over as He departed the next morning to go to Jerusalem.

Meanwhile many worshipers had arrived in Jerusalem to celebrate the Passover. When they heard of the startling event in Bethany, quite a number must have decided to go there and find out for themselves what had really happened. But when they learned that Jesus was on His way to Jerusalem, they returned, running, to announce the news: "Jesus, who raised Lazarus, is coming."

The chief priests were highly displeased at the resurrection of Lazarus. Never mind that a miracle had taken place and that a grieving family had been gladdened. Jealous and angry at Jesus' popularity and His unconventional teachings and actions, they plotted to kill Him, and return Lazarus to his grave also. Jesus knew that He was placing His life in jeopardy by going to Jerusalem, yet He steadfastly set His face toward the fulfillment of His destiny.

In due course, the two large crowds on the road that day met: one group accompanying Christ from Bethany and the other coming from Jerusalem to meet Him. Those from Jerusalem carried palm branches in their hands; and that was the origin of the day we now celebrate as Palm Sunday. Matthew and Mark tell about the crowd that left Bethany with Jesus. They cut down branches from the trees and spread them on the ground, along with their garments, to honor Jesus (Matthew 21:8, Mark 11:8).

What joy and enthusiasm when these two groups met! Together they sang, *"Hosanna to the son of David: Blessed is he that cometh in the name of the Lord; Hosanna in the highest."* The words of this hymn are taken from Psalm 118:25, 26, to which they added certain words demonstrative of their own feelings. The word *"Hosanna"* in Hebrew means "save us" or "save now," and corresponds to the first two words of Psalm 118:25. It was not so much a prayer as an appellation ascribing power to Jesus, and expressing the desire of their hearts for liberation.

This ascription by the crowd had three characteristic motives. The first was political. The Jews at that time were living under Roman rule. Their leaders didn't dare raise their heads against their captors, but the common people who studied the prophecies were expecting the Messiah to come and

13

bring about their political redemption. Even the disciples of Christ thought He was going to establish an earthly kingdom and expected to be given positions of leadership in that kingdom.

The second motive of the crowd was for social reform. In the person of Christ they saw a social reformer, a philanthropist. He had multiplied the loaves and fishes to feed the multitude. He healed the sick and raised the dead. This, they thought, was exactly what their society needed, someone who would look after their temporal welfare.

The religious motive was weakest with the people, but the strongest with the Lord. A political leader would have entered Jerusalem sitting upon a horse or riding in a chariot. But Christ didn't choose these symbols of political victory and worldly triumph (Proverbs 21:31, Jeremiah 17:25, Hosea 14:3). He chose a donkey, thus symbolizing that he was not about to satisfy the shortsighted political and social ambitions of the Jews or of His disciples. He was entering Jerusalem to lay down His life and shed His blood for the sins of the world.

It was true that Christ was going to establish a kingdom, but it would be in the hearts of those who accepted His sacrifice for their sins and acknowledged Him as Savior and Lord. The entrance of Jesus into Jerusalem on a donkey was the fulfillment of the prophecy in Zechariah 9:9: *"Behold, thy King cometh unto thee: he is just, and having salvation; lowly, and riding upon an ass, and upon a colt the foal of an ass."*

Christ could have been acclaimed King that day by the eager multitude. But, had He condescended to become a political and social deliverer, He would have defeated His whole purpose for coming into the world, which was to deliver men from their sins and to occupy the throne of their hearts.

A Christian in name only once flippantly remarked, "I have made Christ my King, but only as a constitutional monarch. I continue to be prime minister." Christ doesn't want to take a second place in your life. He wants you to yield Him the right of absolute authority. Are you willing to let Him?

Something No One Dares to Tell You

When you're expecting important company at your house what happens? The womenfolk bustle about, cleaning, cooking, and setting things to rights. The menfolk shave and put on a clean shirt—maybe even a tie and jacket. If it's a rich relative you expect, his or her picture is prominently displayed in the living room. Everybody's on their best behavior.

But let me ask you a very frank question. What kind of home do you have when company isn't there? Does it have a loving, pleasant atmosphere, or a censorious, faultfinding one? Is it a bit of heaven on earth, or a living hell? Does company like to come to your house, or do they dread having to visit you? Remember, your home is what it is to extent because of what you are. Be honest about it— because a very important Guest is knocking at your door, as He did once long ago at a home in Bethany.

This particular home was very important to Jesus Christ, for it was the dwelling place of His dear friends, Mary, Martha, and Lazarus. Their loving hospitality made it a little bit of heaven on earth to Him. If Christ were to come to your town, would He choose your home in which to stay? If you know in your heart that your home wouldn't be a place of refreshment to Him in body and spirit, then you'd better invite Him in as your Savior and Redeemer. Let Him begin with you. If it's your disposition that's been souring the home atmosphere, He can radically change all that. I've seen home devils become angels of mercy through the transforming power of Christ. Receive Him as your Savior and He will begin to work in your home, your church, your town. You need to become a Mary, a Martha, a Lazarus, so that your home will be a congenial dwelling for Christ. He doesn't care what kind of furnishings you have, or whether you live in a mansion or a single room. What He seeks are hearts that He can make His throne.

It was six days before the Passover when Christ went to Bethany for the last time. Before Him was the prospect of the cross. The burden of His soul was indescribable. Next day—the first Palm Sunday— He would be entering Jerusalem and hailed as a King. Yet, because He would refuse to become a political and social reformer, He knew He would just as quickly be rejected by many who welcomed Him that day. This was the gateway to the suffering that awaited Him in Jerusalem. He knew, however, that the cross would not be the end, that it would be followed by the resurrection. The Master of life would prove that He was indeed the Giver of life.

But before entering upon this last dramatic week—in which He would experience the popular acclaim of Palm Sunday, the shame of the cross, and the glory of the resurrection—Christ felt the need of the fellowship and warmth of a friendly home. And so He went to Bethany where, in one of His last earthly acts, He showed that He was indeed a man like us, though without sin. As God incarnate, He would one day sit upon a kingly throne, but as man facing a lonely prospect of suffering and death, He found it restful to sit in a well-worn chair in a hospitable home.

But why do you suppose Christ went to the home in Bethany and not to His mother's house? We don't know. It may be that among His kinfolk He would not have found the understanding and acceptance of His coming sacrifice. They might not believe that He would permit His enemies to crucify Him. Perhaps they were skeptical of any talk of His resurrection. They may have reasoned that, since He had the power to perform miracles for others, He would not hesitate to use it for Himself. How shortsighted and blind one's own family can be! To them it might have seemed more logical for Christ to prevent His crucifixion than to endure all the shame and agony of a criminal's death and then cause His resurrection.

This is how man always thinks. He prefers to

escape pain, suffering, and the cross. He can see no good in them. But God thinks otherwise. He considered the cross the necessary prelude to the resurrection. Think back. Would it have been a greater accomplishment for Christ to avoid the cross or to rise from the grave? Which would bring more glory to God and hope to mankind? Perhaps because His own family could not see eye to eye with Him on this, Christ may have preferred to go to Bethany to the home of Lazarus.

This was a home that had already been tested as Christ was about to be tested. Lazarus had also died, bringing heartbreak to his sisters, since they knew that Christ could have saved him. While he was seriously ill, they had sent messengers to Christ imploring Him to come and heal their brother. But Christ had delayed His coming, and when He arrived Lazarus had been dead four days.

What disappointment Mary and Martha had experienced! There may have been a sob of reproach in Martha's voice as she said, *"Lord, if thou hadst been here, my brother had not died"* (John 11:21). We always long for our loved ones to be exempted from evil, sickness, and death. That's as far as our small minds can envision their good. We can only consider the immediate welfare of our families, not the eternal issues involved. Lazarus' sisters could not look ahead to the resurrection. And even if they did think of it, they had no thought of it as the immediate solution to their problem.

How do you view death? Do you think of it as the

final enemy that puts an end to all your aspirations? Or do you see it as the great liberator from the material bonds that have kept you tied down and prevented your achieving your highest potential? Which would you prefer: never to die, ot to die in the expectation of being resurrected? Would you like all eternity to be a mere extension of the present, or do you hope for something better? Technology and science can give no answer; they stop at the gate of death. The speculations of philosophy cannot give any certainty to your anxious heart. To know the things that lie beyond yourself you need light, a revelation that comes from outside yourself. Such light comes only from Christ.

Of course, Christ could intervene to prevent all sickness and death. Why, then, doesn't He do it in answer to your anguished prayers? It's because your health and life are not the highest priorities in His concern for you. Understand this and you will not be angry when God doesn't interfere to heal every bodily ailment that comes your way. If you consider your bodily comfort as the highest good in your life, you will have no hope of the resurrection. You cannot anticipate it with joy if you have not first experienced a spiritual resurrection here and now.

If you have never received Christ as your Savior, you are a walking dead man. Sin has killed you. That is why so many people never think of God or of the possibility of the resurrection. In your last illness, no one dares to remind you that you are going to die. The doctor may inform your relatives, but he will seldom tell you. However, the Great Physician tells you in His Word that *"It is appointed unto men once to die, but after this the judgment"* (Hebrews 9:27). Sooner or later you're going to die, and it's far better, far wiser, to face it now and prepare for it than to wait until the last moment. Only God knows when that will be. But the sooner you prepare to meet death the more you will enjoy life. Paradoxical? Not really. Facing reality and dealing with it brings a sense of relief and release that leaves you free to cope with more important matters. Running away or hiding from unpleasant truths leaves you with a gnawing anxiety that robs life of its zest.

Go to Bethany. Ask Mary and Martha which they would have preferred—that their brother should never have died, or that he should have been resurrected. I'm sure they would tell you the latter, for it brought them a joy, a hope, a certainty that would illumine any suffering and hardship they might have to endure thereafter. If you only knew the joys of life in Christ! Receive Him as Savior and come alive in your spirit. He will transform you and take away the fear of death.

Are You a Victim of Mass Psychology?

You may bear the name of Christian. But when did you really become one? Your answer may be, "I was born a Christian." That's how it goes today. People who happen to be born into a Christian tradition and environment take it for granted that they are Christians, even if they have no idea whatever about Christian doctrine and never practiced Christianity. Those who are born into a Muslim tradition consider themselves Muslims, and so on.

A newspaper editor in Greece once told me, "As far as I am concerned, my religion is going to church from time to time on a Sunday, lighting a candle, and standing by other worshipers—and that's it." And she thought that this gave her the right to call herself a Christian.

Such people attach only secondary importance to personal communion with Christ, to the study of the Word of God, and to a life in accordance with the precepts of Christ. Christianity has degenerated into a formality and a tradition rather than a living fellowship with Jesus Christ. This is why "religion" today means nothing. You can be religious and yet lost.

Someone gave a sundial to a group of people in the jungle. They regarded it as a fetish and wanted to keep it holy, so they built a house over it to keep it safe. This of course, kept the sun away from it. They had rendered it useless by trying to protect it. They beatified the sundial, but they made it of no practical use. That's how many people regard Christianity. It has become something they've enclosed within the beautiful walls and stained glass windows of cathedrals, but which they've walled off from their own individual daily lives. They genuflect to a statue or kiss an icon of a saint, but they fail to imitate the personalities behind these symbols.

Have you ever wondered what became of that great crowd which cheered the Lord Jesus Christ as He triumphantly entered Jerusalem on Palm Sunday? The people had heard that Jesus was coming. His fame had spread everywhere. Just a few days previously He had raised Lazarus of Bethany from the dead. Such news spreads with lightning speed, especially since Bethany was so close to Jerusalem. Who could have ever expected that the One who was being cheered on Palm Sunday would be crucified by the people of Jerusalem in a few days? The enthusiasm of the crowd as they spread palm branches before the little colt that Jesus was riding was not something that had been organized and planned. It was spontaneous, unpremeditated. It may be that one from among the happy crowd had begun to cheer the Lord Jesus and the rest followed suit. Did the crowd stop for a moment to think what it was all about? We all know how easily the masses are led. It has developed into a whole science, called mass psychology. You can lead human beings in crowds even more easily than you can lead sheep. You may have seen this in political gatherings and demonstrations, and you know what I'm talking about. Rarely does an individual exercise individual judgment and discipline during such mass demonstrations. The soul of man gets fired up with emotion and enthusiasm. It all happens on the spur of the moment. Convictions are drowned out by the psychology of the masses.

That's exactly what happened on Palm Sunday. And we are really not much different as we celebrate Palm Sunday with palms in our hands. We do it because everyone else does it. Aren't we like the masses of Jerusalem, who one moment shouted, *"Hosanna: blessed is the King of Israel that cometh in the name of the Lord,"* and shortly thereafter cried, *"Crucify him, crucify him"?* Pilate asked them, *"You who were cheering Christ just a few days ago, tell me, whose life do you want me to spare, that of Jesus or that of Barabbas?"* And the crowd shouted, *"Crucify Jesus, crucify Jesus!"* Is it possible that such words came out of the same mouths that had previously shouted "Hosanna"? Unfortunately, yes. The individuals in both cases had been caught up in the crowds.

Why don't you get away from the crowd for a couple of moments? Forget your mass tradition and what the majority of people do and think. Instead of exercising mass psychology, exercise individual psychology for a change. Think as an individual. What do you as a person isolated from the rest of the world think of Christ? Is your religion the echo of what the masses do and say or is it your own individual conviction? Do you by your own life one day seem to be saying "Hosanna," and on another day say "Crucify him"?

The Man Who Could Have
Avoided Death but Didn't

From the human standpoint He had everything to live for. The common people were eager to acclaim Him as their King. If He had said the word, thousands would have rallied under His banner. He would have been a popular hero. If He had thrown His lot in with the leaders of His own people, kowtowed a little to them, buttered them up a little they would probably have backed Him up in a struggle to overthrow the tyranny of Rome and restore the Kingdom of Israel to the Jews.

Instead He had antagonized them by speaking out against their hypocrisy. Instead of calling for social and political reform, He had demanded inner purity and unselfish love for God and man. He laid bare their greed and double-dealing in public, and they gnashed their teeth in fury and plotted to kill Him.

The religious rulers had gathered together under the leadership of Caiaphas to take counsel against Him, and Christ knew it. And so, before walking into their net, He went by Himself somewhere southeast of Jerusalem to pray and prepare Himself for the ordeal of the cross. Then quietly and with absolute calmness of heart He began His journey to Jerusalem. He well knew that the uphill road would lead to the hill of Golgotha, where He would lay down His life for the sake of a sinful world.

His well-meaning disciples tried to dissuade Him from going. But when they saw Him start out resolutely toward Jerusalem, they didn't have the heart to leave Him alone. This was a critical hour in the life of their Lord. Mark describes the incident graphically: *"And they were in the way going up to Jerusalem; and Jesus went before them: and they were amazed; and as they followed, they were afraid"* (Mark 10:32).

Let us glance first at Christ and then at His retinue. Christ is walking toward Jerusalem with the full realization of what is going to happen. If this were any of us, we'd steer clear of the town where death awaited us. But Christ went forward with true heroism. Usually we avoid speaking of the heroism of Christ, because He was not a hero in the human sense of the word. Christ was God. But at the same time He was man. He took upon Himself flesh; He became man so that He could redeem sinful man. He came to this world for the purpose of serving with His life

30

and saving by His death. As God He could have escaped from those who were going to crucify Him. He could have thwarted them, mocked them, and crushed them. Instead He walked resolutely toward death.

Self-sacrifice is closely connected with the heroism of Christ. He was born for the unique purpose of dying. The cross was the goal of His life. He wasn't throwing His life away; He was fulfilling His purpose. His death was completely voluntary. Regardless of the pressure exerted by enemies and friends, He died because He chose to die. Neither Caiaphas, nor Annas, nor Judas, nor the Sanhedrin, nor Herod, nor Pilate, nor the nails, nor the cross, nor anyone or anything else actually killed Jesus. There were only two nails that kept Him on the cross: His love for us and His obedience to the Father.

A prisoner facing the date of his execution, a mother or father facing the death of a child, or you and I facing some impending disaster, tend to become increasingly anxious as we agonize over what lies ahead. The hours seem to drag out; it would be almost a relief, when hope is gone, to have everything over and done with. As man, Christ also agonized in view of the cross. He considered it necessary to be baptized in this agony, but He wanted it to be over and done with as soon as possible. Scripture tells us, *"And Jesus went before them."* He was in a hurry. Since He was about to die, let the inevitable happen quickly.

How Jesus must have suffered in His humanity!

31

On the one hand He was facing the physical agony of crucifixion, on the other He was impelled forward by His divine will. Human weakness could not overcome divine strength and purpose. The agony of the cross made Him walk toward it with a faster pace.

Although Christ was accompanied by His disciples on this last journey to Jerusalem, He was really alone. His disciples followed in the rear; but as Christ looked forward He could see only the cross. Actually a great gulf separated His thoughts from those of His disciples. He envisioned the blood that would flow from His side to atone for the sins of the world. The disciples were speculating on who among them would occupy first place in His kingdom. For three years these men had lived with Him, yet they still failed to understand what He had come to accomplish. They showed Him so little sympathy.

Never was anyone so alone as Jesus. The disciples' love could not stand the test of the crucifixion; their desertion became nails for His soul at the most critical moment of His life. In death, Jesus was alone. And do you know why? So that you and I, through faith in Him, need never be alone, either in this life or at the hour of death.

How reassuringly the words of Christ ring in our hearts, those last words before He ascended to the Father after His resurrection: *"Lo, I am with you alway, even unto the end of the world"* (Matthew 28:20). Were He less forgiving, He might have added, "in spite of the fact that you left Me alone."

Now consider the disciples' frame of mind as

they walked to Jerusalem. *"They were amazed . . . they were afraid."* The word translated "amazed" is *ethanboumto* in the Greek text, which comes from the same Greek root as *taphos,* "grave." Both words come from the Sanskrit root that means "to render immobile." The disciples were frozen with astonishment and fear as they watched Christ marching quickly toward the cross. It was a dumfounding experience to witness His heroism, self-sacrifice, pain, and loneliness. They finally stopped to consider the meaning of His walk.

You, too, had better stop to think seriously of the meaning of the cross. Why did Christ die? Does His death have any personal meaning for you? Do you possess the eternal life that He came to gain for you through His death? Are you missing the greatest gift God can offer you—pardon and peace through the sacrifice of His Son on your behalf? Stop and think.

The Question You Can't Escape

A Japanese nobleman who came to America once visited a Sunday school to study its function. The superintendent asked him to say a few words to those present. Now this visitor was a Confucianist, and he began by saying that the teachings of Confucius and Christ are just about the same. There are very few differences, he said, and therefore he regarded Christians as brothers.

When he had finished, a distinguished merchant, a member of the Sunday school, rose to his feet. Of course, he recognized the moral teachings of Confucius, he said, but added the following: "There is, however, a basic and vital difference between Confucius and the Lord Jesus Christ. Confucius is dead and remains in his grave until Jesus Christ will raise him. But the tomb of Christ is empty. He lives and He will not see death again. He is in our midst this hour of our Sunday school."

This is the difference between Christ and all other religious leaders. He is God, while all others, no matter how distinguished their teachings, have been only men. The Bible calls Christ *"the Word,"* and declares that *"the Word became flesh"* (John 1:14). Christ, who was born in Bethlehem and lived on this earth for thirty-three years, was a human being like us, but without sin, either hereditary or personal.

Jesus Christ made some bold claims concerning His deity, omnipotence, and eternity. If someone today were to claim to be God, He would probably be considered ready for a mental institution, if he were not already there. Hardly anyone would believe him. He would be asked to support his claim by doing something supernatural, something no one else had ever done.

In the past there have been men who claimed they were born of a virgin. They thought this would bolster their claims to deity. But they never proved their claims by rising from the dead. Yet the Apostle Paul categorically declares that Jesus Christ proved Himself the Son of God in power through the resurrection from the dead (Romans 1:4).

We have indisputable historical proofs concerning the resurrection—proofs that Christ, who appeared in Bethlehem as a human baby, was at the same time the Creator of the universe. He had no beginning and He has no end. Your life and mine

36

began when we were conceived. But Christ was eternally pre-existent as God before He became man in a supernatural manner through the virgin birth.

He died, not because He could not avoid death, but because that was the very purpose for which He came to earth. And one of the reasons for which He died was so that He could rise again from the dead, something that would attest to the certainty of His deity and bring the hope of the resurrection to all who would identify their lives with His.

But more basic for our faith is the fact that Christ was not only *"of the seed of David according to the flesh"* (Romans 1:3), but that He was God. When He became man, He did not cease to be God, and because of this His resurrection as a man was possible. If He were not God, He could not have risen. And because all other religious leaders were only men, their bodies are still in the grave.

Perhaps you are thinking that you can't believe in the resurrection of Christ because it can't be scientifically proved. But there are many things in nature that you accept, yet they remain inexplicable. One of the greatest atomic scientists of the 20th century, Dr. Wernher Von Braun, declared: "Today, more than at any other time, our survival—yours and mine and that of our children—depends upon our dedication to moral principles. Only ethics will decide if atomic energy will be an earthly blessing or the source of our total destruction or the total destruction of humanity. But where does the desire for ethical behavior originate? What is it that makes us

37

desire to be moral? I believe that there are two powers which motivate us. One is a last Judgment, when each one of us will give an accounting as to how he has used the great gift of life which God has given us on earth. And the second power is faith in the immortal soul, in the soul which will rejoice for the reward or that will suffer the punishment which will be imposed at the last Judgment.

"Therefore, faith in God and in immortality gives us the moral power and the moral direction which we need for nearly every action of our daily life. In our modern world many men seem to think that science has rendered such religious ideas anachronistic. But I think that science presents a real surprise to the unbelievers. Science, for instance, tells us that nothing in nature, not even the minutest matter, can disappear without its trace remaining. Just think of this for a moment. And once you think of it, your thoughts about life will never be the same. Science has discovered that nothing can disappear without its trace remaining. Nature does not know extinction—only transformation.

"Now if God applies this basic principle for the minutest and least important part of His nature, is it not logical for us to believe that He also applies the same principles as far as the tide of His creation is concerned, the human soul? I believe that it is logical. And everything which science has taught us and continues to teach us increases my faith in the continuation of our spiritual being after death. Nothing disappears." (Translated from an article appearing in a magazine in Greece.)

Therefore, is it not illogical to believe that it is possible for our restricted minds to understand how God became man and rose from the dead? The only explanation for the resurrection of Christ is that it is humanly unexplainable, because it was caused by an infinite and eternal God.

Through this same power, God is going to raise us all one day—some to the resurrection of life eternal, a life of unending joy, and others to a resurrection of judgment and eternal punishment. Whether your personal resurrection will be a fearful thing to look forward to or something to rejoice over will depend on your decision to reject or accept Christ as your Savior.

> What will you do with Jesus?
> Neutral you cannot be.
> Some day your heart will be asking
> "What will He do with me?"

Have You Made Up Your Mind about the Resurrection?

A Mohammedan and a Christian were discussing their religions and had agreed that both Mohammed and Christ were prophets. Where, then, lay the difference? The Christian illustrated it this way: "I came to a crossroads and I saw a dead man and a living man. Which one did I ask for directions?" The response came quickly, "The living one, of course." "Why, then," asked his friend, "do you send me to Mohammed who is dead, instead of Christ who is alive?"

This is the basic difference between Christ and every other religious leader. All the others came into the world, lived, and died—but none of them lived again. The resurrection of Christ was the one event that persuaded His disciples once for all that He was indeed God in the flesh and not just a man.

When the Apostle Paul refers to the death and burial of Christ in I Corinthians 15:3, 4, he cites these two events as the prerequisites of Christ's resurrection. *"For I delivered unto you first of all that which I also received, how that Christ died for our sins according to the scriptures; and that he was buried, and that he rose again the third day according to the scriptures."*

Paul declared that the resurrection proved Christ was the Son of God: *"And declared to be the Son of God with power, according to the spirit of holiness, by the resurrection from the dead"* (Romans 1:4). Neither Christianity nor the Church of Christ would have been established or perpetuated if the disciples of Christ hadn't believed absolutely in the deity of Christ. His death and burial didn't produce this certainty. Others had died and been buried, but only Christ arose never to see death again. The cross brought crushing disappointment to the followers of Christ, but the resurrection crowned the cross with the glory of salvation.

Paul doesn't say that *Jesus* died, was buried, and arose; he says this of *Christ.* Why not Jesus instead of Christ? Because Christ is the name that indicates the work He came to accomplish. The name Christ means "The Anointed of God." It comes from the Greek verb *chrio,* which means "to anoint," usually in a sacred sense. His coming into the world through the Virgin Mary, His life, death, burial, and resurrection were not the products of chance; they were

42

foreordained by God for the salvation of man.

When the Word of God says, *"Christ died, was buried, and rose again,"* it is not the same as if this were said of any one of us, as, for example, "George died and was buried." What gives value to these three basic facts about Christ is that they were the fulfillments of very definite prophecies. The phrase, *"according to the scriptures,"* is added repeatedly. Has there ever been anyone else who dared prophesy that he was going to die, then raise himself after three days to prove what he was saying? To anyone who dared to make such a claim we would have to say, "Words are cheap. Prove it."

I believe in the verbal inspiration of the Scriptures. Therefore the words used in the Greek text are very important in arriving at the meaning of these three basic facts concerning the person of Christ as Paul describes them.

When he speaks about the death and burial of Christ, he uses the verbs in the aorist tense: "He died" (*apethanen*), "was buried" (*etaphee*). The aorist tense refers to a historical event of the past. His death and burial are finished. These are historical events that can be proved and that no one can doubt. But the verb Paul uses to refer to the resurrection, *egeegertai*, is in the perfect tense, which refers to historical events of the past that continue to demonstrate their effects and results in the present. Christ was raised and He continues to live today and to live forever.

The Apostle Paul wrote these words about 25

years after Christ's crucifixion and before the Gospel narratives were written. Bible students do not doubt the genuineness of I Corinthians, and it is here that we find the truths generally believed throughout the Christian community around A.D. 55, even though some Corinthians who had been influenced by Greek philosophy doubted them. The objection of others, however, was not based on their inability to prove this historical event but rather on their inability to imagine that anyone could be raised from the dead.

They reasoned this way: The resurrection is not possible; therefore Christ did not rise. Paul is trying to make them think logically. Too often we begin with an *a priori* idea, arbitrarily decided upon, and then reject historical events because they don't agree with what we've decided to believe. We'd certainly be in trouble if our scientists rejected the conclusions of their experiments in favor of their *a priori* ideas. It's the same as if you were to say, "Man can never reach the moon," even though you saw it portrayed on TV. Our forefathers believed it impossible to send a man into space, but now this has been experimentally proved. To reject what we see, of which we have become personal witnesses, is most unscientific. We can't let our prejudices take precedence over the observations and conclusions of our experiments.

"Christ has risen," Paul told the philosophizing Greeks of Corinth. "He is with us now. He lives today. Many have seen Him. In fact, in one instance, over 500 people saw Him at one time." And he adds something very significant: "The majority of these

44

witnesses are alive today." They were undoubtedly scattered throughout the known world by then, but it is as if he were saying, "Go and ask them."

Those who objected to the resurrection would have had to interrogate these witnesses in order to shake or settle the historical authenticity of the resurrection, they stubbornly adhered to their predetermined philosophy that "such a thing is impossible."

Is it possible that such an outmoded, unreasonable *a priori* idea keeps you from facing not only the risen Christ but also the living Christ, the One who can give you resurrection life and eternal life, the One who can make you what neither you nor others believe possible—a new creature, indwelt by God in Christ? Receive the risen, living Christ into your life and you, too, will live.

The Man You Can't Avoid

It was Sunday evening. One of the greatest events of history had taken place. Jesus Christ, who had been crucified and buried, had risen from the dead. The first to learn about this was Mary Magdalene and she went to tell the disciples. Then Peter came to the tomb to see what had happened. And later two travelers on the road to Emmaus were joined by a third man to whom He later revealed Himself as the risen Christ.

The disciples greeted the rumors of the resurrection with mixed emotions. Some believed and some doubted. Perhaps they were discussing this very thing as they talked in whispers behind locked doors in the room where they had congregated. They realized that those who had crucified Jesus would be looking for His followers also. They knew the religious leaders of the people were determined to put an end to the spread of Christian teaching, first by getting rid of Christ, and now by exterminating His disciples.

Such difficult times often serve to bring Christians together. May the various fears through which we Christians go, serve to unite us today, inspite of our differences. This is not a plea for overlooking the cardinal doctrines of the faith in order to achieve a fellowship based on mutual tolerance of error, but a plea for all born-again Christians to unite in a stand against the enemies of the faith.

The disciples had made one basic mistake, however. They thought that closing and locking the doors would assure the security they desired. But neither locked doors nor protective walls can insure protection against our enemies. Our security doesn't lie in material means but in our spiritual weapons, offensive and defensive—the whole armor of God.

In spite of the dangers we face, the door of communication with the outside world must always remain open. Our peace of soul in the face of the hatred of our enemies and their passion to exterminate us is what will attract the world to the Prince of Peace. The spirit of service must stand higher in the life of the Christian than considerations of personal safety. Christ could have shut the door of communication with the outside world and thus have avoided the cross, but in doing this He would not have become the Redeemer of the world. The cross was not His end; it was the zenith of His glory. And if it becomes necessary for us to die for Christ, let us not think this will be the end of our service for Him. It may well be the coronation of our service. Let's not shut our doors. The world can do nothing to us unless God permits it.

Shutting our doors proves that we lack the inward assurance that must always characterize the Christian. This is why the first word Christ spoke to His disciples after His resurrection was *"Peace be unto you"* (John 20:19). He knew that the disciples were disturbed. And He knows that when we shut our doors securely against the world we demonstrate that we too lack peace.

The disciples could never have imagined that Christ would enter the room while they were gathered there with the doors shut. It was not even necessary for them to open the door for Him. He could enter with the doors closed. But why did He? Couldn't He have knocked at the door like anyone else, tell them who He was, and ask them to open up? Of course He could. But He wanted to show them that He was indisputably the risen Christ, the same miracle-working Lord with whom they had lived for three years.

Humanly speaking, it was impossible for any man to enter the room with the doors closed and locked. Only God had such power and ability. And if we are logical, we will concede that it is impossible to impose any restriction upon an eternal God. He who created everything could appear wherever He wanted, and as He wanted. It was the same Christ, with the same characteristics of His human form that He possessed before His burial, though as always fully God, who entered the room.

The sad thing was that without realizing it the disciples had shut the door, not only against their enemies but also against Christ Himself. Sometimes when we shut out the enemy we also shut out Christ. And when we lose our contact with Christ we lose our peace. Our attitude toward our enemies affects our attitude toward Christ. If we hate them, it is as if we hated Christ Himself. If we fear them, it is as if we feared Him. Fear of our enemies deprives us of the peace of Christ in our hearts, and this shows in the agitation with which we face our enemies. The closer the Christian is to Christ the more fearless and serene he will appear in the presence of the enemies of Christ.

In spite of the fact that the disciples had shut out their enemies, and along with them had unconsciously shut out Christ, He entered and stood in their midst. This kind of action, characteristic of Christ during His earthly ministry, is also His practice in this present dispensation of grace. Men try to avoid Him, but He cannot be sidestepped. He bumps into them when they least expect it. Men did not realize then, nor do they now, what Christ can do for them. He seeks them because He knows that only through their meeting with Him can they find the peace they need.

Man seeks peace yet tries to avoid the only One

who can give the real peace that passes all understanding. They think He is dead, and like the disciples on that Sunday evening after the resurrection they shut the door. But He enters their hiding place wherever they are. The love of Christ is without measure for the human soul disturbed as a result of sin. Such disturbance is far more dangerous than men realize. It is the true enemy of their lives, against which Christ wants them to shut the door of their hearts when He comes in to give them the victory.

The Bible tells us that one day Christ came to the region of the Gergesenes, where He encountered two demon-possessed men coming out of the graveyard. They were so wild that no one dared pass that way. When they saw Christ passing by, instead of rejoicing that God had come among them in visible form, they screamed out, *"What have we to do with thee, Jesus, thou Son of God? art thou come hither to torment us before the time?"* (Matthew 8:29). Even though in their crazed minds they rejected Him, Christ freed them from the demons that tortured them.

You may not be as disturbed as they, but you may have very little inward peace. In your fear you may have closed every possible door, every possible window, through which Christ could enter. That is why your condition is so desperate. But you cannot avoid confrontation with Christ. He can come in and make Himself known to you, saying "Peace be unto you." Right now your heart may be closed. Your

51

mind may be shut. But Christ is unavoidable. He speaks to you now. Are you going to accept His offer of peace? He wants you to have it. Are you going to accept the salvation He has provided for you? You cannot lose your fears or become eternally blessed in any other way. Once you experience the peace of the risen Christ, you will wonder how you could ever have been so foolish to shut Him out of your heart and life so long.

An Autopsy

Maybe you've heard it said or maybe you've said it yourself, "I don't believe anything I cannot prove right myself." No one can deprive you of the right to believe only what comes within the range of your experience. But is this always smart?

There was a man just like you. When he heard someone speak about the reliability of the Bible, he became angry, saying, "We cannot accept any book today without knowing who wrote it and that he is trustworthy." A Christian turned to him and asked, "Do you use the multiplication table?" "Of course I do," was his immediate answer. "And who discovered the multiplication table?" "I don't know." "But still you use it, don't you, simply because your teacher taught you the multiplication table." "I use it," replied the unbeliever, "because its practical value has been proven."

"And has not the practical value of the Bible been proven?" No answer came from the unbeliever.

It isn't that God refuses to prove whatever you want to have proven. Many times, however, He doesn't do it because He knows ahead of time what your motives are for asking. What is your motive when you submit all kinds of questions to God? If it is simply to satisfy your curiosity, God will refuse to give you interpretations and revelations. He does not cast His pearls before swine. You don't do that either. If you were a teacher, whom would you want to teach, those who constantly made fun of you or those who would humbly listen to you and judge the value of what you had to say in order to accept it or reject it?

In this connection, we are faced with a very interesting fact. After His resurrection, Christ did not appear to any of His enemies. He appeared only to His disciples and other believers. Why? Why didn't He appear to Pilate, for instance, and say, "Here I am! I told you that no one could take away my life." He could have done it, but He didn't. This is the privilege of omnipotence—the right of selectivism in the demonstration of His power. You and I don't have such a privilege. We do what we must, what we are forced to do. We are limited by our incapacities.

One more thing. If you and I had been in Christ's place and were able to rise from the dead, probably we would have gone to show off to our enemies what we'd been able to do. It's human to show off our achievements. But the opposite is characteristic of deity. And thus Christ, at the hour of His triumphant resurrection, did not appear to His enemies but only to His friends.

His resurrection, however, was a surprise for all, friends and enemies alike. Full of fear, His disciples were hiding in a closed room (John 20:19). They didn't believe that the One whom they saw dying on the cross would rise again. But they had already believed on Him as their Messiah, their Lord, their Savior. And because they had honored Him in the past when they heard His call, He now honored them in His post-resurrection revelation.

The Lord loves to confirm men's faith. The enemies of Christ tried very hard to prove that He had not really risen from the dead. Instead they proved themselves to be stupid. They bribed the soldiers who were keeping the body of Christ to lie, saying that thieves had come and stolen His body while they were asleep. If they were asleep, how did they know that the body of Christ had been stolen? What a transparent lie! Thus we see that the theory that the body of Christ was stolen was only a conjecture. And had it been stolen, wouldn't they have exercised every effort to find it? What liars they were! No matter how many times Christ might have appeared to them, they wouldn't have believed. What He had said and done was enough for them to accept Him for what He claimed to be.

The fact of the resurrection of Christ can be proven to anyone willing to examine the evidence, just as Christ could have proved His resurrection by appearing before His enemies. But such proof would do no good. Christ knew that He had nothing to gain or lose. Five hundred people saw Him at once after his resurrection. And in A.D. 55, when the Apostle Paul wrote to the Corinthians concerning this appearance of Christ after His resurrection, at least half of these 500 people were still alive. The resurrection of Christ is a proven fact. There is history to back it up. What you need, however, is not proof of the historicity of the resurrection of Christ, but the faith to say with Thomas, "My Lord and My God." He does not merely say, "The Lord and the God," but *"My* Lord and *My* God." Is he *your* Lord and *your* God? To Thomas He gave the privilege of autopsy. Why? Because he had already received Christ and had allowed Him to cleanse him from sin. He had already believed on Him. What Christ had said in the Beatitudes became a reality in the life of Thomas, *"Blessed are the pure in heart: for they shall see God"* (Matthew 5:8). God is accessible to all, but only those who believe can see Him. Yours is a faith after an historical autopsy. You believe that Napoleon lived at one time, but you can't see him. Nevertheless, you believe the historical witness of those who saw Napoleon. Christ, however, is the only historical personality who, if you believe on Him, becomes yours and saves you from the guilt and power of sin.

The Condescension of Majesty

With whom do you like to associate? Do you avoid those who are poorer and socially lower than yourself and seek out those who are richer and higher on the social scale than you? If I knew that, I'd have a good insight into your character.

What was Christ's conduct in this respect? Read the New Testament carefully and you'll find that He never looked at people with contempt. For the poor and suffering ones He had pity. When He looked at the great and mighty of this world, He didn't regard their wealth and status, but He knew them for what they were. Rich or poor, Christ did not come to support those who were confident that they could manage their own lives. Self-confidence is sometimes the enemy of faith. Yet what are our accomplishments when compared to those of our Creator?

Christ rose from the dead. This is something that no one has ever been able to achieve for himself. If He had been an ordinary man, naturally He would be very proud of His achievement. But He was both God and man, and as such His basic characteristic was one of humility. Most of His disciples saw Him after His resurrection. One, however, did not, and that was Thomas. He was reluctant to accept the testimony of others. "I must see Him with my own eyes," he reasoned, "in order to believe it. I must touch His side and His hands so that I can become personally persuaded that it is the same Christ whom I knew before He was crucified."

If you were in Christ's place, what would you have done? Would you have condescended to have Thomas touch your resurrected body and then accept his testimony, or would you have said, "Who is this Thomas who desires to touch My body? Whether he believes or not makes no difference to Me. I don't need Thomas." This is man's attitude in general, but not God's. Man is egocentric. To him, no one is greater and more important than himself. He wants to accomplish the goal that he has set for himself. He wants to earn his living; he wants to achieve something; he wants to ascend the ladder of success. His basic interest is not in others but in himself. God, however, is an altruist. The center of God's interest is not Himself, but others—you and I. He sets in motion a whole universe in order to save one man, to persuade him that he is the object of His care and love.

And He speaks to him in a language he can understand. One of the miracles of the majesty of God is that He makes His majesty accessible to us.

Christ knew where Thomas was to be found that night. He didn't wait for Thomas to come to Him to be persuaded of the fact of the resurrection. Christ took the initiative and went Himself. This is the great condescension of deity. God does not wait for unbelief to seek Him out, but He goes out to rescue unbelief and turn it into faith. It is not man who takes the initiative in the matter of his own redemption, but God.

The greatest discovery that you can make in your own life is that Christ is interested in you. It is not you who knock at His door, but He who knocks at yours. You hide in fear, but He finds a way to enter the hidden recesses of your heart in order to persuade you that He loves you and is personally interested in you.

I once received a letter from a woman in Thessalonica which said: "It was impossible for me to realize that I, a little grain of sand, an insignificant woman among the millions of people, would be honored by a visit from God Himself in the person of Jesus Christ. May the Lord help you to take me out of the maze of doubt and unbelief. I have always loved my Lord since childhood but it was a nebulous love. I felt pity for Him because they crucified Him. Now, however, my mind is clearing and my life is becoming calm as a result of His personal intervention in my life. Before, I used to call upon Him, but it seemed I could never reach up to Him. Now, however, I realize that He has reached down to me. My elevation has been the result of His condescension. He has filled me with joy that I never knew before. I confessed my sin and the burden of my soul rolled away."

This is the miracle Christ performs in a human life when anyone meets Him personally and accepts His invitation to come to Him. On your own initiative, you can never go to Christ. You can never reach up to Him. You must accept His reaching down to you. You must recognize that there is nothing you need more than Christ and His salvation. You, too, must echo Thomas' confession, "*My* Lord and *my* God." For of what use is a God who is not your very own?

A poor German girl announced that she was going to give a piano concert. In order to attract people to come, she mentioned in the advertisements that she was the student of the famous Hungarian professor, Franz Liszt. But it was a falsehood. To her dismay, she learned that on the day before the concert the professor was going to visit her town. What should she do now? She went to meet him, confessed her guilt, and asked him to forgive her. The professor answered, "You made a mistake. All of us make mistakes. The only thing that you can do now is to repent; and I believe that you have already repented. Sit down and play." At the beginning, she played with much trepidation. The professor corrected a few of her mistakes and said, "Now truly you can say that I taught you. Go ahead and play at your concert tomorrow evening, and the last piece will not be played by you, but by your teacher."

You are like this girl. You have sinned. There is nothing else you can do but repent. And then you will play the role of your life under the supervision of Christ Himself. The last and the best piece will be played by Him.

The Cure for Doubt

Doubt is not always bad in itself. In fact, if you doubt something, it often proves that you are thinking. It would be wrong to condemn all who doubt without examining the reason for their doubt.

Even among the disciples of Christ there was one who became known as "doubting Thomas." The world is full of doubters. But not all have the same reasons for doubt. The value of doubt depends on its motive.

Some people doubt because of indifference. They are not interested in the things of God and therefore make no attempt to resolve their doubts or try to find the truth by going to the source of truth, God's Word.

Others doubt because of pride. They consider themselves so much more intellectual or discerning than others that they're not willing to accept anything that would cause them to acknowledge they could possibly be wrong.

A third kind of doubter is the analyst, the sincerely perplexed individual who doubts because he finds it difficult to accept something he hasn't seen or experienced. There are honest agnostics. But despite their sincerity they may be confused as to what constitutes proper criteria for judging the truth of a matter. They went to examine the kingdom of the spirit with their bodily senses.

Let's stop for a bit to consider what kind of doubt Thomas had. It seems he was a bit shortsighted where faith was concerned. We know that in order to see a man must have eyes. However, not all people have the same kind of eyesight. Some are farsighted, others are nearsighted; some can see easily, others with great difficulty. The eyes of the soul are similar. One man can see divine truth more readily than another.

Thomas believed, but with hesitancy. Many of us are like him in this respect. We lack the spiritual perception to recognize Christ at once. It takes us longer than others to say, "My Lord and my God." Three times in the Gospels Thomas is quoted, and each time his sorrow is apparent.

The first instance is when Christ, condemned to death, went to Judea. His disciples sought to restrain Him. But Thomas turned to them and said, *"Let us also go, that we may die with Him"* (John 11:16). A man who was willing to die with Christ cannot really

64

be condemned as an unbeliever.

The second instance is when Christ was speaking to His disciples during the last supper. He told them that they could not follow where He was going. Thomas was perturbed at this and said, *"Lord, we know not whither thou goest; and how can we know the way?"* (John 14:5). Thomas loved the Lord very much and he wanted to follow Him under all circumstances, no matter where that led.

And the third instance is when Thomas spoke with Christ one week after His resurrection. He had just expressed reluctance to believe without proof, as though the news of Christ's resurrection were almost too good to be true—and he did not want to have his hopes dashed by believing prematurely. But didn't the others who actually saw Christ as soon as He was risen show the same kind of hesitation?

Thomas was not a hypocrite. In all sincerity he expressed the question marks that were in his mind. And Christ understood him perfectly, just as He understands each one of us. After all, as God He created us. Therefore He knows that each one of us is different from every other person. To you who long to believe and cannot, I say, Don't give up. God will meet your need if you come to Him sincerely seeking light. Like an ophthalmologist, He doesn't prescribe the same kind of glasses for everybody. It all depends on your spiritual vision. The weaker your eyes the stronger the glasses. To the weak He gives greater strength so that they can see as well as the stronger ones.

Why wasn't Thomas in that first meeting of the disciples on the Sunday after the resurrection? It may have been that he was too utterly cast down. He may have stayed away in order to weep out his sorrow alone. His doubt arose in his heart long before his meeting with the risen Christ. It sprang, not from an unbelieving heart, but out of love that grieved to see the object of his love suffering.

When the Lord discerns that the motive of our unbelief is not an unwillingness to accept Him, but a longing to be convinced if we honestly could, He volunteers to take our finger and place it on the nailprints in His hands and the wound in His side, as it were. He lovingly meets the need of the willing heart.

No matter what kind of doubts you may have, don't hesitate to approach the risen Christ with them. Your contact with Him will bring a change in your life; it will make you a new man or woman; it will make you cry out in faith like Thomas, "My Lord and my God."

Do You Really Want to Know?

People can often be cruel and unreasonable in their judgments. They brand others as heretics, unbelievers, or "heathen" without making any effort to understand them.

Take Thomas, for instance, often referred to as "the doubting disciple." A whole week after the crucifixion he still had not seen the resurrected Christ. The other disciples reported they had seen Him, but Thomas was skeptical. Then one day Christ entered the room where the disciples were gathered— entered through a closed door! And Thomas was shaken. Was this really Christ or a phantom?

Thomas may have heard the rumors that were going around—all sorts of wild speculations. Some may have claimed that the body of Christ had not risen, but only His spirit, as the Jehovah's Witnesses of our day believe and teach. They follow in part the errors of Docetism, a heresy that refused to recognize that Jesus Christ had a real physical body. The Docetists claimed that those who saw Him merely thought that He possessed a human body. Their name comes from the Greek verb *dokeoo*, "to believe or imagine." They even went so far as to claim that Christ thought He had a body without really having one. And the Jehovah's Witnesses try to persuade us that Christ's resurrection body was imaginary, thus explaining how He was able to come into a room through closed doors.

If it weren't for Thomas's skepticism we might not be able to refute this nonsense. But Thomas doggedly insisted that he would not believe unless he could actually touch the nailprints in Jesus' hands and feet, and the place where the sword had pierced His side. He wasn't doing this out of a desire to be controversial or argumentative. No, he was deadly in earnest about proving something that was a matter of life and death to him. His basic need was to solve the question of whether Jesus Christ had actually risen from the grave. Was His resurrection real or imaginary? Was it a physical or merely a spiritual resurrection? Who can see a spirit with his physical eyes or touch it with his hand? That was the test—the only test—that would convince Thomas—the evidence of his senses.

It is unfair to Thomas to call him an unbeliever. Rather, he was of an investigative turn of mind.

68

Christianity would be in trouble if it were not for those who insisted on investigating the grounds for belief. Christianity is not a religion of unreasoning faith. Why should Thomas remain forever in doubt about Christ's physical resurrection? Why should he also commit us to remain in doubt? One man's investigation can become the foundation for the faith of many. Thanks, Thomas, for your investigative spirit.

In order to do justice to the character of Thomas, let's look at three events in the New Testament that shed light on his relationship to the Lord Jesus.

The first was his heroic offer to go to Jerusalem to die with Christ. We find this recorded in John 11:16: *"Then said Thomas, which is called Didymus, unto his fellowdisciples, Let us also go, that we may die with him."* He was ready to give his life for His Master and Lord.

The second instance occurred in the upper room, when Christ told the disciples, *"Whither I go ye know, and the way ye know"* (John 14:4). Thomas asked, *"Lord, we know not whither thou goest; and how can we know the way?"* (v. 5). He was never afraid to resolve his doubts by saying what was in his mind. His question elicited one of the most important statements Christ ever made about Himself: *"I am the way, the truth, and the life: no man cometh unto the Father, but by me"* (v. 6).

And the third instance occurred when Christ appeared to His disciples a week after His resurrection, and Thomas was invited to touch Him to prove that it was indeed Christ in the flesh that had risen.

What loving condescension Christ showed in allowing Himself to be thus investigated! Would you tolerate such a challenge of your credentials? If you, as a father or mother, were challenged by your child to prove that you were really his parent, how much tolerance would you have shown? Probably very little. After all, you and I are human and inclined to resent any imputation that we are not what we represent ourselves to be. Christ is God and is not afraid of being investigated. Anyone who comes to Him eager and willing to have his doubts resolved and removed will find Him more than willing to help. He was not afraid of Thomas's question and investigation, nor is He afraid of yours. But all the hammers of impious doubt and investigation will be broken on the Rock, which is Christ.

In fact, Christ took the initiative in inviting Thomas to examine Him. He knew Thomas had declared to the other disciples, just one week previously, *"Except I shall see in his hands the print of the nails, and put my finger into the print of the nails, and thrust my hand into his side, I will not believe"* (John 20:25). When Christ finally appeared in their midst, Thomas didn't say anything. He was probably too startled and overwhelmed. Then Christ said to Thomas, *"Reach hither thy finger, and behold my hands; and reach hither thy hand, and thrust it into my side: and be not faithless but believing"* (John 20:27).

Christ takes the initiative with any who have honest doubts. Come, He tells you, investigate Me. Don't jump to conclusions without proof. No scientist reaches conclusions without making the necessary experiments. Christ wants you to make this experiment. Take Him at His Word and try the salvation He offers. Try it on His terms: repent of your sins; tell Him you're willing to believe with all your heart; promise to follow where He leads. If you lose anything, I will share your loss. But if you are the gainer, you must sacrifice yourself along with me in order to make Him known to others.

Christ didn't reveal Himself to Thomas just to satisfy his curiosity. He knew that Thomas had been willing to die with Him, and that once convinced he would be willing to live for Him.

You and I are more blessed than Thomas, because we can base our faith on his investigation. *"Blessed are they that have not seen, and yet have believed,"* said Christ. May you, too, be found among those whom Christ blesses.

Seeing Is Believing

To Christians all over the world, Easter has always been the holiest day of the year. The early Roman Christians used to call it "the joyful Lord's Day." When they met each other on the street, their usual greeting was the same as that which the Greeks exchange at Easter: "Christ is risen!" And the response, "He is risen indeed!"

Of course, many people don't believe in the resurrection. A Christian listening to a group of highly educated people discussing religion was surprised that they couldn't accept the historical proof of the resurrection. "Excuse me," he said, "but I am sure Christ rose from the dead. I believe it, not just because it's historically proven, but because I've experienced it personally. This morning I spent an hour with the risen Lord. I spoke to Him, and He spoke to me."

To him, his inner communion with Christ was the greatest proof that the Lord had risen. If you're not living in vital fellowship with Him, then your attendance at church on Easter is just a matter of custom, without any spiritual benefit to you whatever.

It's true that the miracle of the resurrection is beyond human comprehension. It's just as mysterious as life itself. Life is the synthesis of certain material elements and the influence of a supernatural non-material power over them. Matter wihout this divine element can never become a seeing, moving, hearing, thinking body-personality that has the ability to relate to God Himself.

Though no one actually saw Christ rise from the dead, many people saw Him after His resurrection. The Apostle John recorded the events surrounding this miracle, not only to prove it happened but also to show how the faith of the disciples was developed.

Let's look at the two main events of John 20: Peter and John's visit to the sepulcher, and the visit of Mary Magdalene. These brought about the awakening and assurance of faith to them, after they had seen the risen Christ. But Christ's appraisal of the worth of faith comes in the brief words He spoke to unbelieving Thomas: *"Because thou has seen me, thou hast believed: blessed are they that have not seen, and yet have believed"* (v. 29). "Seeing is believing," says the skeptic. But Christ says that

74

those who believe by faith alone are even more blessed than those who saw Him after His resurrection. That means all who have believed in Him ever since.

Is this unreasonable? Are we supposed to swallow the resurrection story whole simply on some preacher's say-so? No, that's not exactly how one comes to believe or disbelieve. If you want to know whether the Bible account is true or not, you've got to be willing to believe and willing to act on that belief, if you can be convinced of the truth of the resurrection. Then you've got to care enough to examine the evidence—in this case the Bible itself. And then you've got to pray something like this, "Oh, God, if this whole thing is true, bring conviction to my heart, and I'll believe it and receive Christ as my Savior." Otherwise why should God bother to show you at all? Why is faith commended in Scripture? Because it's a response to God's Holy Spirit speaking to your spirit. And why is unbelief condemned? Because it's evidence of a person's unwillingness to open his heart to the Holy Spirit's conviction.

The Bible account indicates that the resurrection took place some time before dawn. At daybreak Mary Magdalene started out with some other women to go to the sepulcher. When she found it empty, she left to report the matter to the disciples. Peter and John ran with haste to confirm her story. Peter, impulsive as usual, rushed right into the tomb. John hesitated, then followed. In his record of this event John acknowledges, perhaps with great shame, his hesitancy. Then he goes on to say, "And he saw, and believed." He confesses his weakness, but he had to see before he could believe. He doesn't pretend to be any better than Thomas in this regard.

Though John believed, he may have had some lingering doubts. His faith had been awakened by the partial view he'd had of the evidences for the resurrection: the empty tomb, the grave clothes and head cloth lying neatly folded. However, no one had yet seen Christ Himself. John's faith would be complete when he had seen Him and spoken with Him.

But the risen Christ appeared to Mary before He appeared to John. Peter and John went home after viewing the empty tomb. But Mary stayed behind to give vent to her grief. Her first thought on seeing the empty tomb was that someone had stolen the body of Christ. Despite His prediction that He would rise from the dead, the empty tomb inspired no hope in her. How many times, we, too, arrive at faithless conclusions. Events that should be hope-inspiring seem to us dark and disheartening. The empty tomb should have filled Mary's heart with hope, but instead her eyes were blinded with tears. She, too, had to see and speak to Christ before she could believe. When that happened, she cried from the bottom of her heart, "Rabboni," "Master." Recognition was sure, and her faith was final.

A skeptic was teasing a little girl who believed in Christ. "You don't really know whom you believe in, do you?" he prodded. "There have been many Christs, you know. Which do you believe in?" "I

76

know whom I believe in," she answered readily. "I believe in the Christ who rose from the dead."

And that's the only Christ in whom we can believe. If He had stayed dead, He wouldn't be worth believing in. His resurrection, the empty tomb, and the fellowship we can have with Him must arouse faith in our hearts. We will "see" Christ only when we receive Him by faith as our Savior and Lord. And this will not be physical sight, which requires no faith, but the conviction of the Holy Spirit, who takes the things of Christ and makes them real to us.

Indestructible Love

It was Sunday morning, and Jesus had been dead for three days. As far as most people were concerned, this was just the end of another chapter in the history of the world. It concerned the teacher of Galilee. People could have said that, although He claimed to be God, He did not manage to prove it. He could not hinder His enemies from killing Him. What a spirit of defeatism must have reigned everywhere during those dark hours during which the body of Jesus lay buried!

It was in such an atmosphere that there were three, or maybe more, women whose love for Jesus was not lessened as a result of His death. Their faith in Him was not diminished. True, they really had no hope that He was going to rise from the dead. Very few, if any at all, expected His resurrection, in spite of the clear prophecies regarding it.

According to Mark, these women were Mary Magdalene, Mary the mother of James, and Salome. They came to the sepulcher early in the morning on the first day of the week. Many mistakenly think that these women came to the tomb in the belief that they were going to find Jesus risen from the dead. However, if this was their expectation, why did they come bringing spices in order to anoint His body? They certainly didn't plan to use these on His living body, but on His corpse. These women, who loved the Lord so much because of the salvation He brought to them, had not had an opportunity to anoint His body after the crucifixion and before His burial, and this is why they wanted to do it now. Therefore they came to the sepulcher with the full expectation that they were going to find the dead body of Jesus.

These women did not have a vibrant faith in the promised resurrection of Christ, but they were possessed with deep love and devotion to the person of the Lord Jesus in spite of the fact that they knew He was dead. Their faith in His resurrection was really weaker than the faith of the disciples, to whom the Lord Jesus Himself had prophetically announced His resurrection.

The women wanted someone to roll the stone away from the entrance to the tomb, not because they expected Christ to come out of the sepulcher alive, but so that they could enter in order to use the spices they had brought.

We can learn a basic lesson from the devotion and indestructible love of these women, when they really did not believe that Jesus was going to rise from the dead. Although they knew he was dead, they came to worship Him. As far as they were concerned, even the dead Lord Jesus was far more worthy of their love and worship than anyone who was alive.

Their indestructible love, however, was recompensed by the renewal of their faith. They didn't mind not using the spices they had brought, because Jesus had risen from the dead. We, too, experience such moments in our lives. Our faith may be wiped out, but it is such a blessing when our love survives. So many times it seems that it is impossible for our holy desires and plans to be resurrected, but we continue to be faithful to our duty. We may feel at times that God has disappointed us. Let us never, however, lose our love and devotion for Him. When we come to tell God, who we mistakenly think is dead, that we continue to love Him and worship Him, we shall surprisingly discover that God *is not dead*, but that He is alive and ready to fill our lives with peace and joy. Our indestructible love for Christ is capable of reviving our faith in the living God.

The son of a preacher once asked his father, "Dad, what's the difference between the cherubim and the seraphim?" The father explained that the word "cherubim" was derived from a Hebrew word which means "knowledge" and that the word "seraphim" was derived from another Hebrew word which means "burning," indicative of the fact that the seraphim were spirits that were characterized by their burning love. As soon as the child heard this, he turned to his father and said, "Dad, I hope that when I die I shall be a seraph, because I would prefer to love God rather than know everything."

The love of these women was indestructible because they had believed on Him while He was alive among them. They already had that basic faith which joined them together with Him. He had become their Savior. They realized that the cross of Christ was the climax of His love toward them and toward mankind.

A modern illustration of this concerns two gentlemen who were traveling together. Before they were separated, one said to the other, "Do you ever read the Bible?"

"Yes, I do, but I do not find any profit in my reading of it. I'm going to be frank and tell you that I really do not feel that I love God."

"Neither did I love Him," answered the other, "but I discovered by reading the Bible that God loved me. And He loves you, too, my friend."

This traveler friend had never thought of that. He began to read the Bible as never before. It didn't take him long to discover that the Bible speaks first about the love of God toward man and, because of this love, we too can love Him. In reality, our love towards Christ does not begin with us but with Him. As John says, *"Herein is love, not that we loved God, but that he loved us, and sent his Son to be the propitiation for our sins"* (I John 4:10).

The love that Christ implants in the human heart never dies. In our spiritual darkness, it is as though we buy precious ointments and offer them to Christ during the dark period between Calvary and the morning of the resurrection. Sometimes it is so dark that our eyes cannot see the sun, but love can lead us in the darkness while we hold the spices in our hands. And when we reach the place where love leads us, we find out that our faith should never have left us, because God is alive!

After the Resurrection—What?

The New Testament relates three outstanding incidents of individuals whom Christ raised from the dead: the son of the widow of Nain, Jairus' daughter, and Lazarus. But no one ever rose from the dead never to die again except Jesus Christ. He is the exception to all the rules that govern birth, life, and death. He existed before He made His appearance on this earth, and He continues to exist to all eternity after having risen from the dead.

Christ's earthly life was divided into two parts: the years from birth to death, and the forty days after His death. Many saw Him during this latter period, so that no one can claim His resurrection was not real. What makes these witnesses especially believable is that it could have cost them their lives to say they had seen Christ alive after Pilate had ordered Him crucified. No one is going to stake his life on something that didn't happen.

Christ's historically attested resurrection is the confirmation of His deity, that He was all He claimed to be. On the day He arose, He appeared first to Mary Magadalene and then to Peter. Later in the day He joined two believers who were walking toward Emmaus. They were wondering what to make of the rumor that Christ was risen. Without revealing His identity, Christ began to expound the Scriptures concerning Himself to them, and finally they realized who He was. Still later He appeared to ten of His disciples who were gathered together. Only Judas and Thomas were missing.

Then for a whole week Christ didn't make an appearance. Doubts concerning the resurrection began to increase, especially in the mind of Thomas, who had not seen Christ. This was perhaps the most trying week for the faith of the disciples.

But the Sunday after the resurrection Christ again appeared to them. This time Thomas was present and had his doubts set at rest. He saw Christ's pierced hands and wounded side and was invited to "touch and see." With what joy, contrition, and wonder he exclaimed, "My Lord my God!" Christ's resurrection will do you no good unless you recieve the risen Savior as your very own. Fall on your knees and say with Thomas, "My Lord and my God!" Christ will forgive you; He will save you; He will make you a child of God.

Christ's third appearance to His disciples was on the shores of Lake Galilee, as described in the 21st chapter of John. On this occasion He addressed some heart-searching words to Peter, fully restoring His relationship with this disciple who had so recently denied his Lord.

His fourth appearance occurred on the mountain in Galilee where He had previously been transfigured. Here He spoke to a gathering that included not only His disciples but also some 500 believers.

His forty days were almost up. The Feast of Pentecost had come. Jews from all over had gathered for this celebration, including the disciples who had returned from Galilee. There in Jerusalem Christ met them for the last time. He guided them to Bethany, and as He lifted up His hands and blessed them He departed from them, going into heaven. In obedience to His command, the disciples returned to Jerusalem to wait for the coming of the Holy Spirit.

These are not all the appearances of Christ during the forty days after His resurrection. But these few will serve to emphasize some basic truths. The first is that during this time the Lord revealed many things to His disciples that they would have found difficult to understand or believe before His resurrection. How wonderfully rich and deep must have been Christ's ministry to His own during this period. It was so full that John couldn't record it all. Immediately after writing of the resurrection he wrote: *"And many other signs truly did Jesus in the presence of his disciples, which are not written in this book: but these are written, that ye might believe that Jesus is the Christ, the Son of God; and that believing ye might have life through his name"* (John 20:30, 31). After His resurrection, the disciples were fully persuaded that whatever Christ said was believable. His resurrection was the seal of His authority and deity.

Another thing we learn is that Christ's body after the resurrection was the same body that He had before death. It was actual flesh and bones. He could eat and drink. Nevertheless, the Apostle Paul tells us, it was a spiritual body, not subject to the laws of nature. It's impossible for us even to imagine what this body was like. Jesus Christ was the same miracle-working God-man, perfect God and perfect man, yet in a glorified body that could never die. And this body, Scripture tells us, is like the one all believers will receive when they, too, are resurrected at Christ's second coming. It will be a very real body, just as Christ's is real, yet no longer subject to human frailty, sickness, and death.

After His resurrection the Lord didn't appear to strangers but only to His own. He wanted to reveal to them the mystery of the cross and tell them about His future work and theirs. You will never understand these truths until you, too, receive Him as your Savior. Then your eyes will be opened, your heart enlightened and you will be able to rejoice over His resurrection, because Christ saves to the uttermost all who come to Him.

What Happens after Death?
Who Knows?

When someone close to us dies, we can't help wondering what has happened to him as a person. Is his spirit still alive somewhere? Will we see him again? We're not satisfied with pious platitudes. We want trustworthy information. Who can give it to us?

Only one person—Jesus Christ, the only One ever to come back from the grave in a resurrected body to give us assurance of life after death. Of course He didn't need to go beyond the portals of death to know what takes place there. But, because He did, we can believe what He has to tell us about the world beyond death.

Christ's knowledge is not acquired, as ours is, but is inherent. In going beyond death, Christ learned nothing He didn't know before. But He went and came back that we might believe what He was going to reveal to us about the after-life. We can believe Him without hesitation or question.

When Nicodemus, that prominent Hebrew religious leader, came to talk to Christ one night, the Master said to him, *"Verily, verily, I say unto thee, We speak that we do know, and testify that we have seen; and ye receive not our witness"* (John 3:11). You see, even when Christ told Nicodemus spiritual truths, Nicodemus questioned them: *"Ye receive not our witness."*

When a child begins to learn arithmetic, the teacher tells him that $2 + 2 = 4$. How much progress would that child make if he refused to accept that truth? Our knowledge, generally speaking, is based on the teaching of others whom we regard as reliable.

Let's apply this to our knowledge about heaven. What do you know about it? Where is heaven? Who lives there? Who will go there? Who knows?

Christ affirmed that Heaven exists. He told Nicodemus, *"No man hath ascended up to heaven, but he that came down from heaven, even the Son of man which is in heaven"* (John 3:13). Heaven was Christ's dwelling place in His eternal state as God. Heaven is also the place of the triune Godhead. We recognize this every time we say, *"Our Father which art in heaven"* (Matthew 6:9). The Psalmist recognized this when he said, *"Unto thee lift I up mine eyes, O thou that dwellest in the heavens"* (Psalm 123:1). Jesus declared that heaven was the dwelling

92

place of the Father: *"Let your light so shine before men, that they may see your good works, and glorify your Father which is in heaven"* (Matthew 5:16). Heaven was the place from which the Holy Spirit descended on the occasion of Jesus' baptism: *"And, lo, the heavens were opened unto him, and he saw the Spirit of God descending like a dove, and lighting upon him"* (Matthew 3:16). Thus heaven is the eternal dwelling place of God the Father, God the Son, and God the Holy Spirit. This is one more indisputable proof of the triunity of God.

But God is present everywhere. How is it possible, then, for Him to have a special dwelling place? We can't place restrictions upon God. He isn't limited by time or space. Human beings can't even think outside the framework of time and space. When we speak of heaven, we can only think of it as a place. But heaven as the "dwelling place" of the infinite God must be thought of as infinite space, if we can call it that.

The Scriptures ask, *"But will God indeed dwell on the earth? behold, the heaven and heaven of heavens cannot contain thee; how much less this house [Solomon's temple] that I have builded?"* (I Kings 8:27). God is in heaven and at the same time present everywhere. He is as near to each one of us as the air around us. *"Am I a God at hand, saith the Lord, and not a God afar off? Can any hide himself in secret places that I shall not see him? saith the Lord. Do not I fill heaven and earth? saith the Lord"* (Jeremiah 23:23, 24). And David asked, *"Whither*

93

shall I go from thy spirit? or whither shall I flee from thy presence? If I ascend up into heaven, thou art there: if I make my bed in hell [sheol], behold, thou art there" (Psalm 139:7, 8).

Christ was trying to explain to Nicodemus things pertaining to heaven. *"If I have told you earthly things, and ye believe not, how shall ye believe, if I tell you of heavenly things?"* He asks (John 3:12). He went on to tell Nicodemus that He alone had descended from heaven to reveal heavenly things to men. No one had ever ascended into heaven to learn heavenly truths and come back to tell them to men. The only One who is entitled to speak of these things is the Son of man who came down from heaven for that purpose.

Until the resurrection of Christ, no one had ascended to heaven with his resurrection body, not even David, as Peter declared in Acts 2:34. Only the risen Christ had done this, and it was then that He carried with Him all the faithful ones of the Old Testament. Before that they were in *hades*, though in a separate section from unbelievers, as Christ taught in Luke 16:19-31. Before Christ's resurrection, believers and unbelievers alike descended into *hades*, which was divided into two sections. But, after Christ's resurrection, believers are never said to descend into *hades*. *Hades* now is reserved for unbelievers. This is brought out in Matthew 16:18, where we read, *"And I say unto thee, That thou art Peter, and upon this rock I will build my church; and the gates of hades shall not prevail against it."* We see that *hades* represents only hatred toward the Church of Christ, and therefore represents only unbelievers.

Heaven, the spiritual-heaven to which Christ ascended (Acts 1:11), is the present dwelling place of the believer. Paul says in Philippians 1:23, *"For I am in a strait betwixt two, having a desire to depart, and to be with Christ; which is far better."* Since Christ is in heaven, that's where Paul expected to go.

Is heaven expecting you? Or is *hades* awaiting you? The decision is yours. If you believe on the Lord Jesus Christ with all your heart, you can be absolutely sure of heaven. If not, you can be absolutely sure of *hades*. And that is hell.

What Is Resurrection?

W e celebrate the resurrection of Jesus Christ at Easter time. But can we, as logical people, believe that a dead body can be resurrected? Let me ask you another question: Did we believe a few years ago that men could reach the moon and actually walk on it? Yet today we have pictures of the moon taken by men on the moon. Perhaps a day will come when someone will colonize the moon. Yesterday's seeming impossibilities have become today's realities. The achievements of science teach us not to be too hasty in concluding that this, that and the other thing is impossible.

A student of that great scientist, Faraday, was greatly distressed because he had accidentally dropped a small silver cup into a solution of nitric acid. Immediately the cup dissolved. "Don't be so disturbed, my boy," said the famous chemist. He took a powder that looked like salt and dropped it into the solution in which the cup had disappeared. The student was utterly amazed when he saw silver once again being formed. After that, he separated the silver and proceeded to make the cup over again. Was this new cup the same as the old one? Yes and no. It was the same in one sense, because the substance was the same. But the shape of the new cup was different, much finer than the previous one.

When we speak of the resurrection, what do we really mean? If we are going to have a new body, what will it be like? Will it be exactly the same body as the one we had in this life? Scripture teaches that it will be the same yet different, just like the new silver cup that Faraday made.

When we speak of the resurrection of the body we don't mean it will be composed of the same cells that constitute our present organism. A lady once said, "How can my body be resurrected intact, since I lost one of my legs in London? It is over there now, and I'm in America, where I most probably will die."

This confused woman didn't think clearly enough. To her it was as if God needed to take a broom to sweep together the cells of her body in order to make a new one out of what remained of the old. Didn't God as Creator make everything out of nothing? Once you accept God as the Creator, you will have no difficulty in believing Him capable of reconstituting your body as He pleases, possibly again out of nothing if the necessity arises. Look at what He has done with us living human beings. We are made up of the same constituent physical and chemical parts, yet each of us is different from the other. Don't you think that the same God can re-make our resurrection body of material that He will form, which will retain the individual distinctions of personality? Scripture teaches that He is going to give us a new body, which will resemble and be recognizable as having the same characteristics as the old. Yet it will be basically different because it will not be subject to the restrictive material laws of the present universe.

When we speak of the resurrection of the body, we do not necessarily mean the reconstitution of the constituent parts of our present body, but the reforming of a reconstituted body in a personality. We as individuals, as personalities, will be resurrected—and not just the cells that make up our bodies. When Mary Magdalene and the disciples saw Christ they recognized Him. He was exactly the same person He was before, but now He could appear wherever He wanted to, without the restrictions of physical resistance. He entered the room where the disciples were while the doors were still closed. He never did anything like this before His resurrection. He wanted to show the difference between what the body in its earthly form can do and what the body of the resurrection can do—a body having the same recognizable characteristics but different capabilities. Here we are not simply discussing the possibility of one theory or another, but we are speaking about historical incidents.

This is why the Apostle Paul, whose mind was far more brilliant than most men's, in writing to the Philippians said, *"For our citizenship is in heaven, from which also we eagerly wait for a Savior, the Lord Jesus Christ; who will transform the body of our humble state into conformity with the body of His glory, by the exertion of the power that He has even to subject all things to Himself"* (Philippians 3:20 and 21; NASB).

Christ did not die for Himself nor did He rise for Himself. Had He not risen, our sorrow over death would be justified, because we would have no hope of our own resurrection, nor could we ever hope to see those who had died before us. Since for all of us death is inevitable, the resurrection should be one of the most fascinating subjects we could study.

The body you now possess is a body of humiliation, says Paul. One day you will receive a body similar to that of the risen Christ. I have no doubt that the proud Greeks did not like Paul's characterization of their body as a body of humiliation. They almost worshiped the human body. To them it was a symbol of beauty. That is why their statues were naked. But the Apostle Paul shouts at the top of his voice that the present body is one of humiliation. It is as if he were saying, "You're going to lose it someday, and you're going to gain another body, a glorious one, similar to the body of Jesus Christ in His resurrection."

But it isn't only believers who are going to rise from the dead. Unbelievers will also rise. All will have new and different bodies—different and yet the same. *"Marvel not at this,"* said Christ, *"for the hour is coming, in the which all that are in the graves shall hear his voice."* This includes believers and unbelievers, but He goes on to say, *"And shall come forth; they that have done good, unto the resurrection of life; and they that have done evil, unto the resurrection of damnation"* (John 5:28, 29). Then there will be no further opportunity of repentance. Your eternal destiny will have been sealed once and for all at that time. Better do something about it now.

Let Christ himself tell you how you can obtain eternal life. You don't have to believe me, but surely you should believe the One who rose from the dead and who knows better than you or I. It will be to your advantage to listen and heed His advice: *"He that heareth my word, and believeth on him that sent me, hath everlasting life, and shall not come into condemnation [judgment]; but is passed from death unto life"* (John 5:24). You don't have to wait for this to happen on the resurrection day. It must happen here and now. Then the resurrection will be a continuation of the life in Christ which He can impart to you right now.

New Bodies

If you place a seed in the hand of a small child and tell him it contains the life of a great tree, will he believe you? It all depends on his faith in your superior knowledge. If a Christian tells a dying man that his mortal body, "planted" in the grave, is like a seed that will one day be raised as a living body, incorruptible, strong and noble, will he believe him? It all depends on whether he has the same faith in God's Word that the Christian has. The tree that grows out of a seed is as nothing compared to the wonderful body of the resurrection. But the point is that God who can do the one can do the other also. He can raise your dead body.

A man who was dying called upon his secretary to write a letter to a friend. "I continue to be in the land of the living," his secretary wrote in her desire to help him. But he corrected her. Instead, he instructed her to write, "I am still found in the land of the dying, but soon I shall be found in the land of the living."

When you die, life escapes from your body. No matter who you are, you're going to go through this. Are you ready? You can live like a king or a pauper, but one thing is certain—you're going to die like a man. Death is where the river of life joins with the great river of eternity. Each Christian upon the face of this earth bids the dead body good-bye, while Heaven welcomes the soul.

Resurrection... It is that candle which cannot be put out by the darkness of sorrow that surrounds death. Let me give you a piece of advice. Light a candle instead of bemoaning the darkness. The candle will shed light upon the pathway of your life and enable you to face the lonely and inexorable moment of death. Death spreads darkness. You cannot dissipate it; only God can do that—through the resurrection of His Son. To you He gives the opportunity to light a candle of personal faith, by accepting His Word that your dead body will one day be raised to new life that can never die.

When we speak of the resurrection of the body, we do not mean that God will go about collecting the remains of your old body. The new body is going to be a new creation. The Apostle Paul in I Corinthians 15:44 calls it a spiritual body. This body will not be mastered by the soul but by the spirit, a fact that

104

characterizes humans only and not animals. Man has a soul as his common possession with animals, which enables him to be conscious of his environment. But the spirit is something that he alone among God's creatures possesses. Our earthly lives are what Paul calls "psychic," that is, they are governed by the soul or the animal instincts in man. But in the resurrection it will be the spirit that will have pre-eminence.

Many people are confused because the Bible sometimes uses the word "soul" instead of "spirit," but never the word "spirit" to refer to the "soul." Sometimes the word "soul" is used to refer to the entire immaterial part of man. Your body connects you with the material kingdom. It is that which pulls you downward. The soul, however, which animates your body, joins you with your environment and with all things living. It is a parallel line of life. But the spirit, which only man possesses, is a vertical line that connects you with the upper kingdom, that is, with God.

The body of the resurrection is changed from "psychic" or "soulish" to a spiritual body. It is no longer governed by the animal instincts but by the spirit. The believer is liberated from both the soul and the earthly body.

Don't consider it an impossibility that God can give you a body that has the same recognizable characteristics as your present body, though with one basic difference. It will not be hampered by the present limitations to which your body is subject. Think about these words of the Apostle Paul:

"But some man will say, How are the dead raised up? and with what body do they come? Thou fool, that which thou sowest is not quickened, except it die: and that which thou sowest, thou sowest not that body that shall be, but bare grain, it may chance of wheat, or of some other grain: but God giveth it a body as it hath pleased him, and to every seed his own body" (I Corinthians 15:35-38).

Do you think that God who created your corruptible yet marvelous body does not have the ability to create the body of the resurrection? Life does not cease to exist. Yes, the present body does cease to exist, but God creates a new body for every one of us. Is it possible that God meant such resurrection life only for the trees, perpetuated through seeds, and not for man whom He originally created in His own image?

Once when Billy Graham was speaking at a large university, some students began to ridicule him. They kept interrupting him with ridiculous questions and boos. He turned to them and said, "The reason you behave this way is because you have many unsolved problems. Your greatest problems are related to death and eternity. I want to tell you about a university girl who died as a result of a traffic accident. Her last words to her mother were, 'Mother, you taught me everything that I needed in order to go through university. You taught me how to light my cigarette, how to drink, how to love without getting into trouble. But, Mother, you never taught me how to die, and this moment has come so unexpectedly. Please, Mother, teach me quickly, because I am dying!' "

Quiet reigned over the audience. If this moment also comes suddenly and unexpectedly for you, are you ready? Jesus Christ said, *"I am the resurrection, and the life: he that believeth in me, though he were dead, yet shall he live: and whosoever liveth and believeth in me shall never die. Believest thou this?"* (John 11:25, 26).

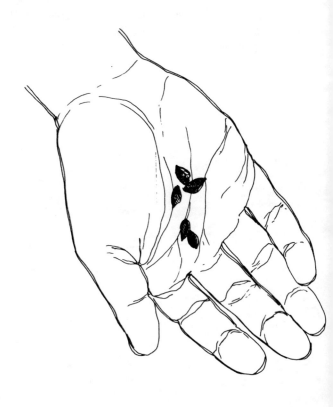

A New Life

$\mathbf{A}$re you fed up with life? If so, it means you need a new life.

Don't be afraid. I'm not going to suggest that you become isolated in some monastery. I want you to come with me to a garden in Jerusalem. Come; examine this garden. You have nothing to lose. If you don't come, your life will remain the same. Your investigation is to your advantage. There is no obligation, but this may liberate you from your present bondage.

If you come with me to Jerusalem you will see the tomb of Christ, but you will not see the dead body of Christ. It is here that Christianity begins. It is not a philosophy like all other religions. Christianity is the living Christ. And, because Christ lives, He gives new life to all those who receive Him as their Savior

Don't look at the resurrection of Christ as a mere historical event that bears no relationship to your life. It may not do so at present, but it can renew your life radically, as it renewed mine when I believed and was born again.

Most people celebrate Easter as a holiday, but not as the event that has given them life. Pay attention to what Paul says in Romans 6:4, *"Like as Christ was raised up from the dead by the glory of the Father, even so we also should walk in newness of life."* Christ was delivered up or died for our sins and He rose for our justification (Romans 4:25).

However, we are speaking about two events that belong to two different realms. The resurrection of Christ was not a spiritual resurrection but a physical one. Many saw the body of Christ after His resurrection. Some touched it with their hands. It is only those who are unwilling to examine the evidence, or who are irresponsible and misinformed people such as the Jehovah's Witnesses, who do not accept the physical resurrection of Christ.

The new life, received when you believe in Christ, is spiritual. When you receive it, it doesn't mean that any physical change will take place in you, but your attitudes and your whole inner self will change. You will no longer pursue sin. Sin may pursue you, but it will not be able to overtake and master you.

The resurrection of Christ was physical. The day will come when you will have a physical resur-

110

rection also. This, however, will happen in the last day, as Paul says in I Corinthians 15:42-54. Your corruptible body will be replaced by an incorruptible one. Whether you want this or not, it will take place. It will happen to both believers and unbelievers. Don't say that this is impossible, because this will indicate a lack of intelligence.

A professor of biology stood before his students holding a seed. He then bowed before the seed. His students were amazed. The professor had spent his whole life studying the origin of things which even to this day continues to be a mystery. He said, "I know exactly the constituent parts of this seed and in what quantities they are found in it. I can take these separate elements and mix them and form a seed that looks like this one. If, however, I put it in the ground, nothing will happen. It will just disintegrate into its constituent parts. This is the mysterious element that we call life."

If you are smarter than this biologist, then *you try* to make a seed that will grow up to be a tree. If you cannot accomplish this, you had better keep quiet and accept the mystery of life. The physical resurrection of Christ is likewise a mystery, and so is your own future physical resurrection. The life that you now possess, which makes you other than a dead body, is also a mystery. He, therefore, who originally created this mortal body, will recreate a new body that will be immortal.

When considering your *spiritual* resurrection, you must request life from God. The source of your

111

physical and your spiritual life is the same. God is the One who works in both worlds. He will raise your physical body in the same manner that He raised the physical body of Christ. It is He who gives you spiritual life the moment you believe the Gospel. As the physical body which is dead is unable to rise by itself, so the soul, dead in trespasses and sins and separated from the Creator, finds it impossible to acquire spiritual life on its own. Eternal life is something that Christ must give and man must receive. The miracle of spiritual regeneration, receiving new life in Christ, is as wonderful as your physical resurrection will be some day.

Don't be afraid that you will not be able to manage your new spiritual personality. It is not you who will live the Christian life, but Christ in you and through you. Your whole nature changes.

"Oh, how much I would have to quit!" thought a sinner to himself as he contemplated accepting Christ. "How much that I now do I would have to give up when I become a Christian!"

"Don't be afraid," a passing Christian said to him. "Are there not many things now that you cannot do? Can you eat mud?"

"No, of course not. I don't even want to eat mud." That's exactly what will happen to you when Christ begins to live in you. The sin which you now desire you will detest then. And if you do not detest it, that will mean that you never really obtained the new life which the resurrection of Christ gives you freely and which you acquire by faith.

The Consequences of Fear

There isn't a single one of us who doesn't dream. And our dreams are sometimes pretty wild. We may dream that thieves snatch our children out of our arms. They empty our wardrobes. But we wake up in the morning and our children are with us in their beds and our clothes are in our wardrobes. It was a dream, we say.

It wouldn't be bad if dreams occurred only in our sleep. But unfortunately we also daydream. We fantasize any number of dangers. What's going to happen to me if I lose my job? What's going to happen if my child gets sick? What if cancer attacks me? What if my children starve to death? These "ifs" in our lives bring more destruction than real sicknesses and difficulties would.

Charles Haddon Spurgeon, that famous preacher of London, was a man with many responsibilities. He was going home after a difficult day, and his problems were so many that he was discouraged. While in this state of mind, however, he was reminded of a verse from the Word of God, "My grace is sufficient for thee." He looked up to God and said, "I believe it is sufficient for today, dear Lord." And then he burst into laughter. He understood how ridiculous it was to worry. He began to think: "I'm like a fish that is very thirsty, who's beginning to worry lest it exhaust the water of the river. The big river answers, 'Drink, my little fish, all you want, there will be plenty for you.' Again, Spurgeon said, "I thought that I was like a little mouse in the great big grain stores of Egypt after the seven years of abundance of harvest, and I was so fearful lest I would die of starvation. At that time Joseph appeared and said to me, 'Don't worry, little mouse, the wheat stores are sufficient for you.' And again I thought that I was someone on top of a mountain talking to himself and saying, 'I'm afraid I'm going to exhaust all the oxygen there is in the atmosphere.' But I heard the atmosphere saying to me, 'Do not be afraid, little man, you breathe all you want. Fill your lungs; there is enough oxygen for everybody.'"

There are two kinds of people who are candidates for heaven. Those who have little faith and those who have much faith. Little faith will take our souls to heaven, but much faith will bring heaven to us. The important thing is for us to begin living in heaven now. In order for us to accomplish this we must stop the sighs produced by the various "ifs" of life and begin to face life as it is.

Doctors tell us that 70% of the people who come to them are not really sick, but they think they are. And it's not too difficult for you to become what you think you might be. Worry over health is one of the first reasons for heart disease.

There was a man who was very anxious about a large debt he owed. His doctor advised him to stop worrying. "How can I do this when my debt remains unpaid? Its weight is so great over my head that I fear it's going to kill me. Your telling me not to worry is like my ordering my cook to tell the water in the kettle over the fire not to boil."

Don't be like that woman who one day felt unexpectedly well. "How are you, lady?" someone asked. "Today I am quite well, but tomorrow I am sure I am going to suffer again," she sighed. It is a terrible thing to expect evil that may never come your way. The expectation of evil kills many more than the evil itself.

Remember the three women, two named Mary and one Salome, who brought their spices to the tomb in order to anoint the dead body of their master? They knew that Christ's enemies had not been satisfied merely to bury his body but had placed a great stone in front of the sepulcher. On the way to the sepulcher the women began to think, "Who is going to roll away the stone?" They knew that they themselves couldn't do it. The stone was extremely heavy. Even if they were men, they probably couldn't do it. When they arrived, just imagine their surprise when they saw the stone rolled away. All their worry was for nothing. A difficulty they had anticipated never happened. They should have believed the words of Christ when He said that on the third day He would rise from the dead (Mark 9:31). *"But they understood not that saying, and were afraid to ask him"* (Mark 9:32). They lacked faith in the resurrection of Christ, and this is why they worried about the stone.

Said the robin to the sparrow:

"I should really like to know

Why these anxious human beings

Rush about and worry so."

Said the sparrow to the robin:

"I'm sure that it must be

That they have no Heavenly Father

Such as cares for you and me."

Let me ask you, is God your Heavenly Father? Don't think that He's automatically the Father of all people. Of course, He cares for all like a Heavenly Father, but only those have a right to call Him their Father who have become His children by faith in Christ. Man has demonstrated no gratitude to God. Instead, he has chosen Satan to be his father. How could you escape worry having such a father? Salvation through Christ is the only way to switch forever the family of Satan into the family of God.

How You Can Become Daring

What do you know about the Sanhedrin of Jerusalem? It was the holy synod of the Jews. It consisted of 70 members plus the presiding officer, the High Priest. Among its members were the Sadducees, Pharisees, and scribes. The Sadducees were in the majority. The people were not without representation before this holy synod. The religious consul, therefore, of the Jews was a democratic governing body, and that's how affairs should be run today. We should not govern the people without allowing them to express their opinion.

The representatives of the people at the Sanhedrin were called counselors. One of them was Joseph. He was an honorable man. I don't know why the evangelist takes the trouble to call him an honorable counselor. Was it because he constituted the exception to the rule? It's quite possible that it was not a very common thing for one to find an honorable counselor. It is almost so today. In the ultimate analysis, we are to blame because we elect these people into positions of leadership.

And what did this honorable counselor do? He went to ask for the dead body of Christ from Pilate in order to give it decent burial. This took quite a bit of courage. It was the Jewish holy synod to which he belonged that had sentenced Christ to death. And now it was really something that one of the members of the Sanhedrin was asking for permission to take the body of Christ and bury it.

He was expecting the kingdom of God. He was a student of the Old Testament. He had followed the life of Christ. He admired Him. Undoubtedly, he thought to himself, this must be the expected Messiah. Nevertheless, he had cast his vote for the condemnation of Jesus. His conscience, however, bothered him. It's a good thing he had a conscience that was still at work. Not too many counselors have a sensitive conscience. It may be that he stood near the cross to see Christ die. He heard His words, which were not outbursts of condemnation for those who were crucifying Him, but words of love and forgiveness. Perhaps he had followed Him during His public ministry as He healed the humanly incurable, raised the dead, and fed the multitudes. His entire life was lived for the sake of others. He had plenty of power when it came to helping others.

Could it be that Joseph thought to himself, "How could He have such power to exercise on behalf of others, and now that He is hanging on the cross fail to exercise it on His own behalf?" Joseph of Arimathea was a man who could think. He could not accept the fact that this Christ who performed such miraculous acts during His life could not do something similar at the time of His own execution. But the question was, "Why did He not exercise the same power on behalf of Himself?"

It was not because He couldn't do it, but because He did not choose to do so. If He were simply a man, He would have exercised His power during His crucifixion. Who is the man who has the power to escape death and would not do it? But Jesus Christ did not come into the world primarily to live, but to die. We come into the world to live, but the principle work of Christ was not accomplished during His life, but during His death. Therefore, if He came down from the cross, He would have failed in the purpose for which He came to this world, and there would have been no means by which you and I could be redeemed.

John tells us that this counselor was a secret disciple of Christ. His discipleship was secret because of his fear of the Jews (John 19:38). When did Joseph become an open disciple instead of a secret one? I have no doubt that it was during the time of the crucifixion of Christ. The iron entered his soul when he saw Christ being jeered at on the cross.

One of the greatest musicians of all times was Handel. He composed the music that portrayed the

53rd chapter of Isaiah. When he reached the third verse, which says, *"He is despised and rejected of men; a man of sorrows, and acquainted with grief,"* he could not go on. He burst into tears. God the omnipotent one on the cross? He could have come down to confound His executioners and yet He did not do it. And sinful man, instead of appreciating this, ridicules Him. Could man have been plunged into a worse degradation than this? The music that Handel soaked with tears of regret for the sinful conduct of man cannot but touch the lives of many people.

Take the time to stand by the cross of Christ, as did Joseph the counselor and Handel the musician. If you do not dare do something as an individual that is different from what the crowd did, it is as if you, too, were giving your consent to the crucifixion of Christ. Yes, you yourself are crucifying Christ. Fall on your knees and confess faith in Him. Believe that He is God in the flesh crucified for you. It may be that until now you have been a secret disciple. Dare to become an open one. Your heart will be filled with indescribable joy.

You must do what a high priest did one day. In spite of the fact that he was holding a high position in a Christian church, he recognized that he had never received Jesus Christ as his own personal Savior. He asked Christ to give him eternal life. He humbled himself. He did not care what his fellow-priests might say. His joy became so great that he witnessed to anyone he met that he now had eternal life. The joy of eternal life becomes real when it travels from your heart to your lips.

A missionary was asked to give a proof of the saving power of the cross. His answer was: "When I arrived at the islands of Fiji my first duty was to bury the arms, the feet, the heads, which had been cut off from the missionaries who were cut up by the cannibals. They cooked their bodies and ate them. But I lived to see these same cannibals who ate human flesh take part in holy communion with indescribable gratitude for the blood of Christ which was shed for their forgiveness."

The changed life that led to the daring of a Jewish counselor to ask permission to be allowed to bury the body of Christ was the result of his facing the cross. You may face the cross, too, with faith, and thereafter receive God's strength to live a daring, fearless life.

The Peace That You Lack

I am dying. Leave me alone. Do not move me. This was the request of a badly wounded soldier. His comrades obeyed him and returned to the battle. After a while, an officer saw this soldier wallowing in a river of blood. "Can I help you at all in anything?" "No, thank you." "Can I bring you a little water?" "No, thank you, I am dying." "Do you want me to write to your home or to any friend?" "No, I have no friends. But you will oblige me if you do something for me. In my satchel you will find a New Testament. Please take it. Open it to the 14th chapter of the Gospel of John. Toward the end of the chapter you will find a verse which begins with the word 'peace'." The officer did as requested and read: *"Peace I leave with you, my peace I give unto you: not as the world giveth, give I unto you. Let not your heart be troubled, neither let it be afraid"* (John 14:27).

No one doubts that we live in a troubled world. Are we human beings condemned to a life of permanent trouble? No matter how hard we try with all our sociological reforms, we don't seem to be able to manage to bring peace to this disturbed world of ours, to our nation, and to our family. Worst of all, however, is our troubled souls, the war that takes place within us. Is it possible for us to acquire inner peace? We need it more than anything else in life.

Sometimes we feel discouraged and separated even from God. We are possessed with fear. Like a cloud, the sense of being forgotten by God descends upon us.

Such a state of mind and heart overwhelmed the disciples after Christ's death on the cross. Our leader whom we worshiped has died, they thought to themselves. They could not understand that if Christ had not died they could not find their own peace of soul, which they needed more than anything else.

But Christ did rise from the dead. That which His friends did not expect or His enemies believe possible took place. And the very same night after His resurrection, He stood before His disciples. They were all taken aback when they saw Him. Was He real or was He a ghost? In order to persuade them that it was He Himself, as they knew Him, He showed them His hands and His side. The first words He uttered were "Peace be unto you." It was as if He were saying, "My resurrection is one more basic reason for you to have peace of heart."

Peace of heart. No physical element can give it to you. You may have good health, fine relatives, a wonderful country to live in, friends and neighbors, but none of these can give you inner peace. True peace of heart is a gift of God. It is the result of Christ's crucifixion and resurrection. It is offered freely to all who believe. Certain special divine gifts are given only to a few, but the peace of God is given generally to all who believe. If you do not have it, that means that you have not yet believed and have therefore not been saved from sin.

All of us retain our personalities when we believe in Christ. Physically, we remain the same. When we're saved, that doesn't mean that our natural abilities will change. We remain what we are, but we can acquire that one basic element and ingredient we so vitally need, and that is peace. All other possessions are of less value.

The word "peace" occurs in the Bible more than 250 times. St. Paul used it more than 40 times when writing from a prison cell. He possessed this peace, which not even incarceration could take away from him. No circumstance of life can affect the peace He gives. The outward circumstances of life cannot give it nor can they take it away. Peace is the sister of the forgiveness of sin, of the grace of God. Christ gives it to you as soon as you make Him your Savior and Lord. As Christ departed from this earth, the last words He repeated three times to His own were, *"Peace be unto you"* (John 20:19, 21, 26).

Is there such peace in your heart? When you go to sleep at night, are you disturbed? The greatest cause of such disturbance is sin. The sinner cannot possibly have the peace of Christ in his heart. *"There is no peace, saith the Lord, unto the wicked"* (Isaiah 48:22).

A girl who was completely given to the pleasures of this world and to acquiring as much education as possible in order to show off, confessed in despair to a friend of hers, "Oh, what I wouldn't give if I could know real peace of soul!"

Peace means harmonious relationships. Peace of soul means a harmonious, friendly relationship between you and your Creator. *"Therefore being justified by faith, we have peace with God through our Lord Jesus Christ"* (Romans 5:1).

A painting of the healing of the two blind men of Jericho was examined by a poet and an artist. The poet observed, "Everything in this picture is worthy of admiration—Christ, the world, the blind men, and so on." But the artist was impressed by only one thing. He said to the poet, "Do you see that cane left behind near the steps of the house? To me, that is the most wonderful detail of this picture. You know what it tells me? That the blind man was sitting on the steps. But, when he heard that Jesus Christ was passing by, he was so sure that he was going to be healed that he left his cane behind him. He knew that he was not going to need it any more." You, too, can leave behind you the crutch or cane on which you have been depending once you get up and follow

Christ. Light and peace will flood your soul as you begin your new walk in the Lord Jesus.

Other Books by Dr. Spiros Zodhiates

Studies on I Corinthians

Studies on Matthew

Studies on Luke

Studies in John's Gospel

Studies on James

Three-Volume Set in handsome slip cover

Miscellaneous Titles

NOTES

NOTES

NOTES

NOTES

NOTES

NOTES

NOTES

NOTES

NOTES

NOTES

NOTES